Dear _____,

Please join us for a howling Halloween Party on October 31st at 7:00 pm! Let's eat, drink, and be scary!

From your trusted hipster friends!

Boho Hipster

Happy Halloween

Coloring Book

Sandy Mahony
Mary Lou Brown

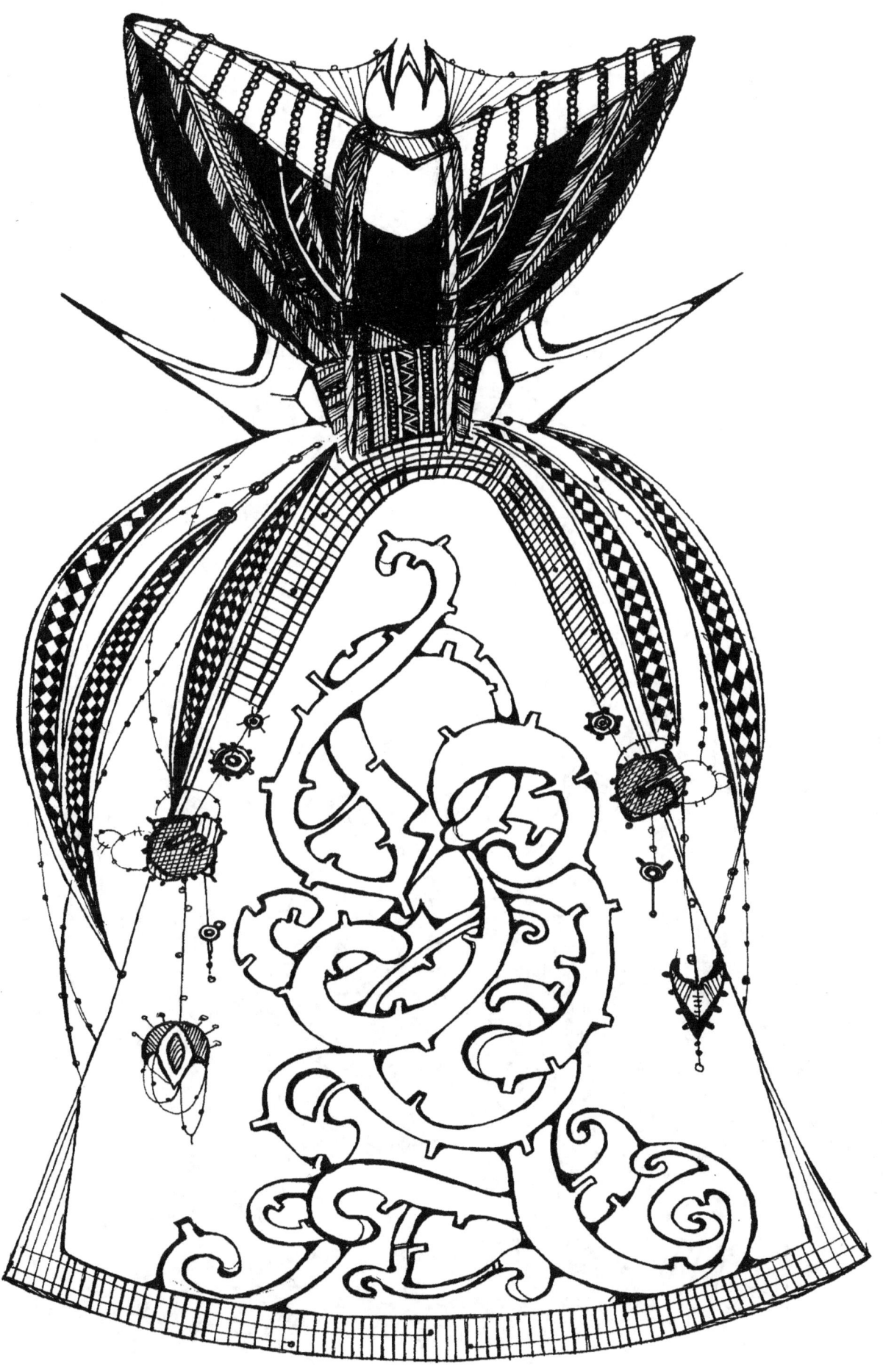

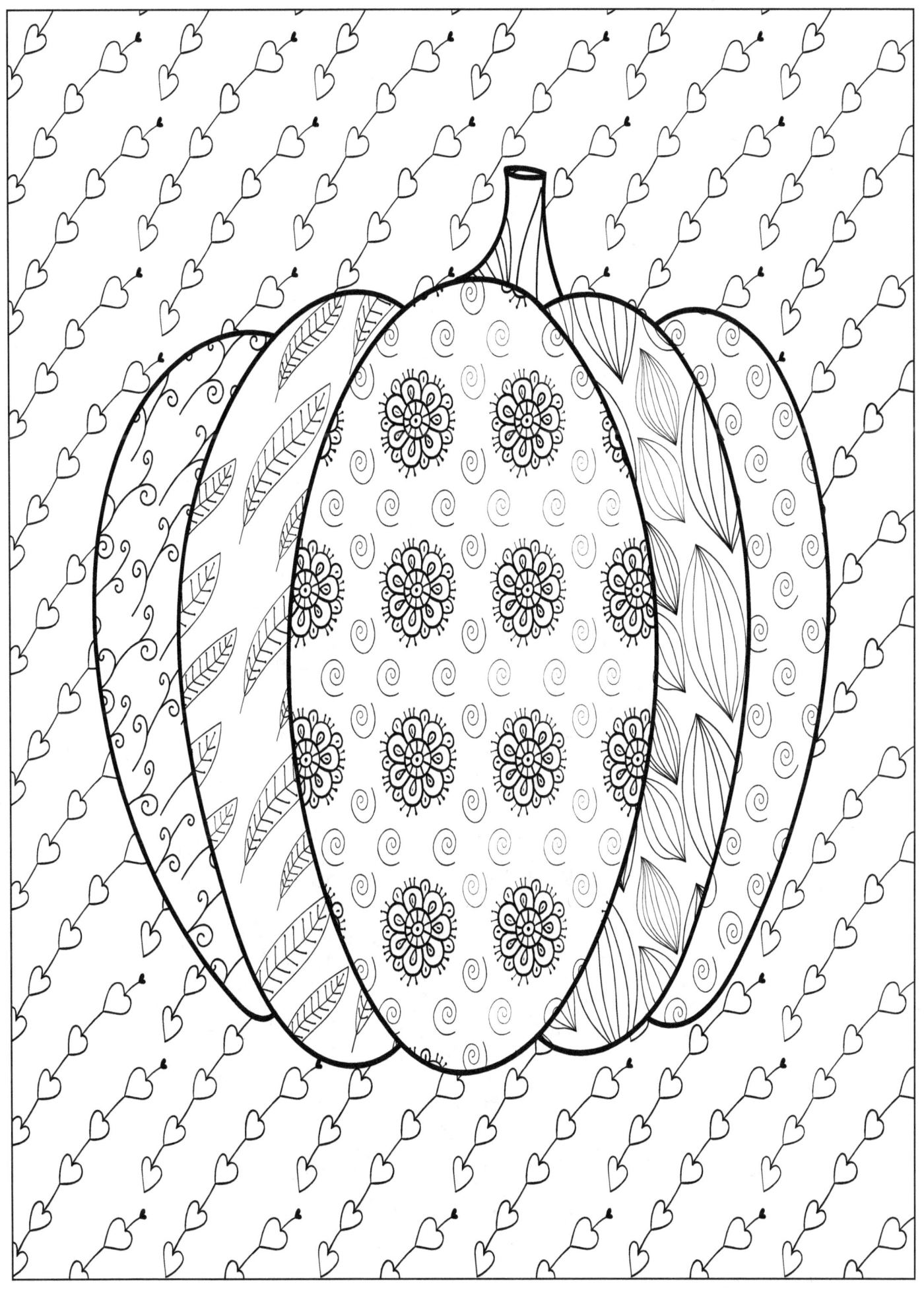

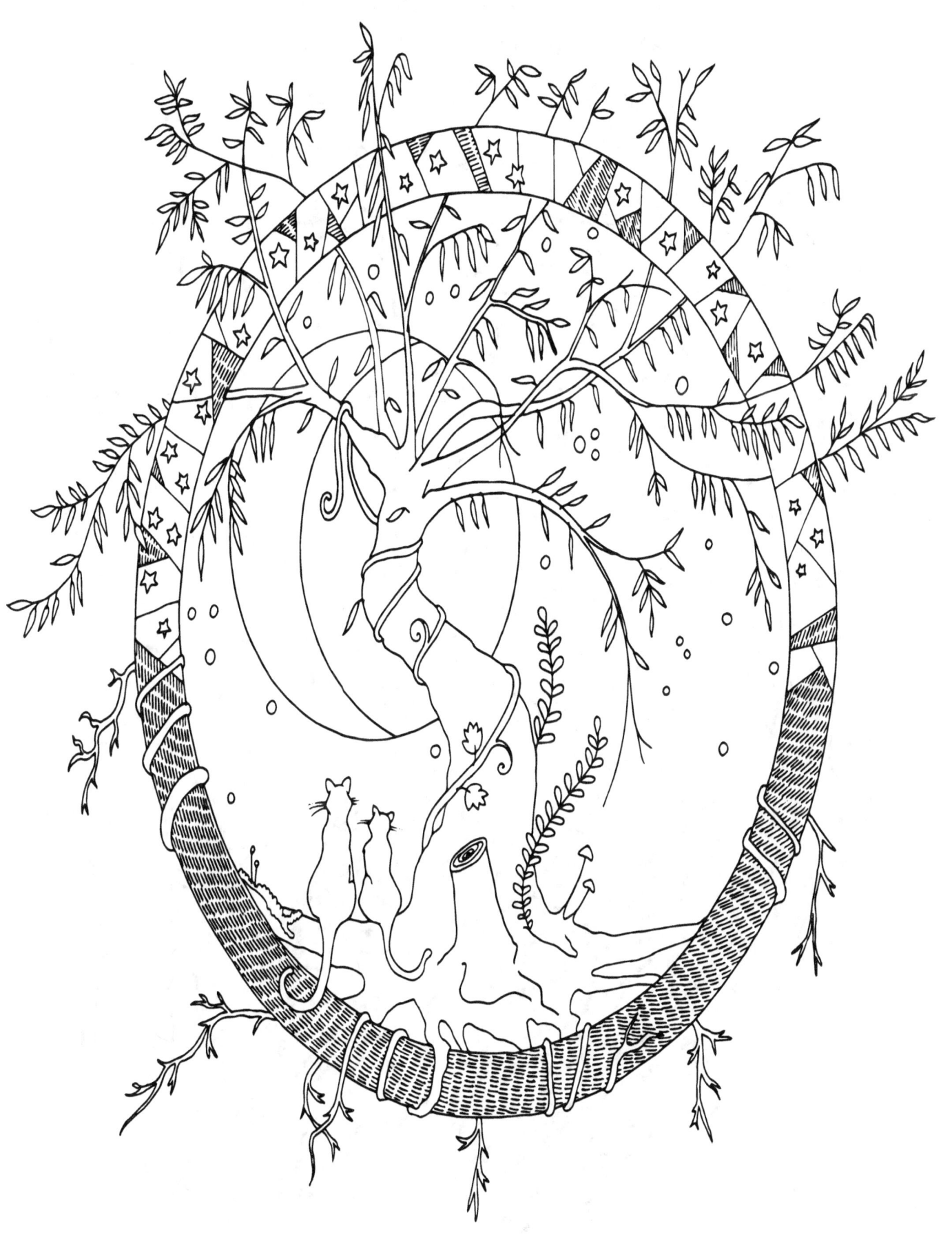

adventurelearningpress.com

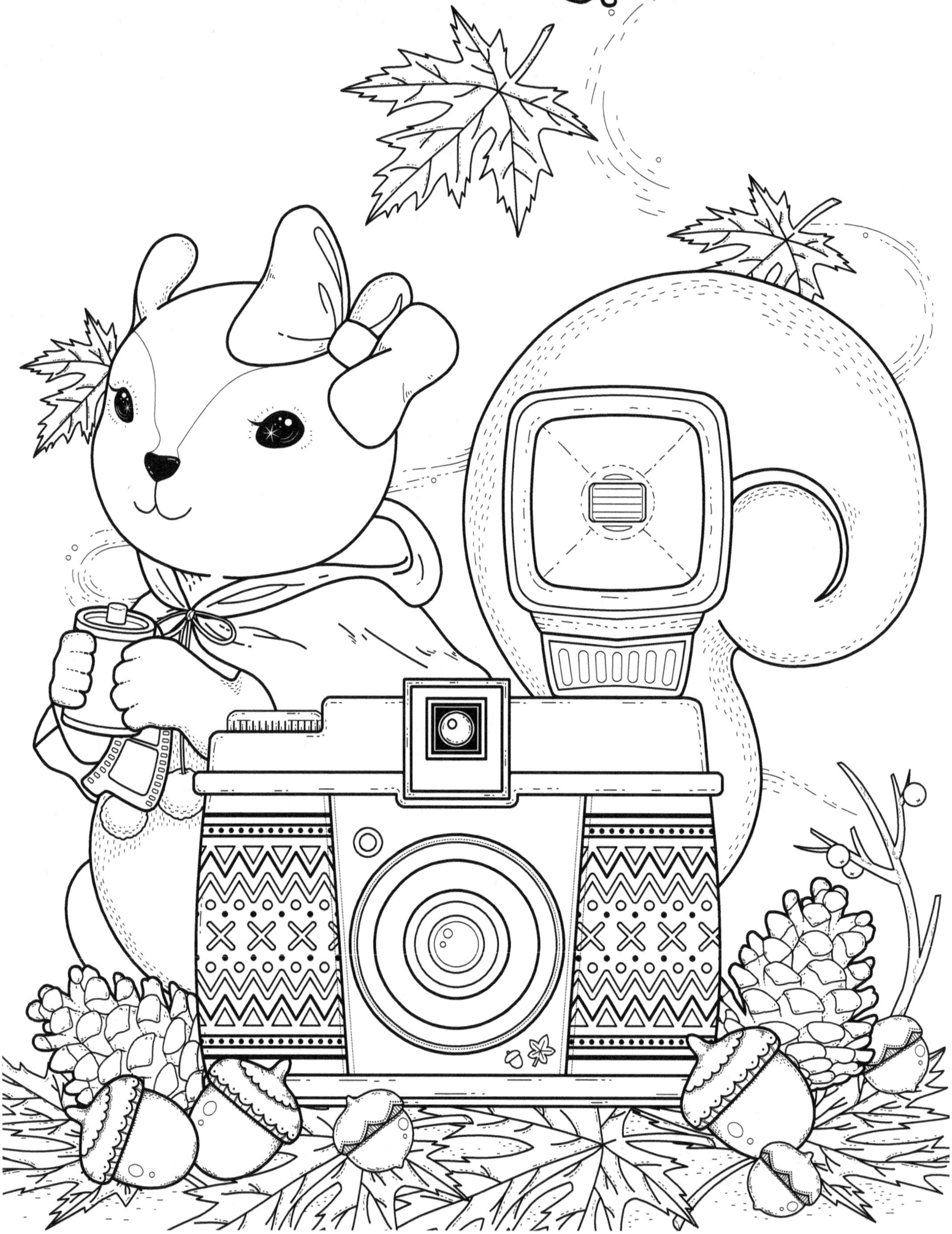